Philip Jodidio

SANTIAGO CALATRAVA

1951

Architect, Engineer, Artist

TASCHEN

HONG KONG KÖLN LONDON LOS ANGELES MADRID PARIS TOKYO

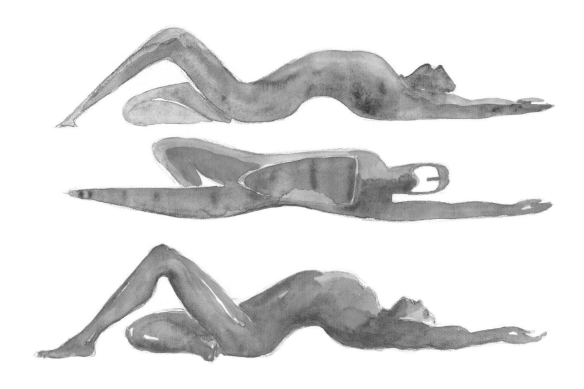

Illustration page 2 ▶ Portrait of Santiago
Calatrava, 1997
Illustration page 4 ▶ Watercolor sketch of human
figures by Santiago Calatrava, 1999

© 2007 TASCHEN GmbH
Hohenzollernring 53, D-50672 Köln
www.taschen.com

Editor ▶ Peter Gössel, Bremen
Project management ▶ Florian Kobler, Cologne;
Katrin Schumann, Bremen
Design and layout ▶ Gössel und Partner, Bremen
Editorial coordination ▶ Sonja Altmeppen, Berlin

Printed in Germany
ISBN 978-3-8228-4873-9

Contents

The Secret of Philanthropy

"I started out wanting to go to art school," recalls Santiago Calatrava. "Then, one day, I went to buy some things in a stationary store in Valencia, and I saw a little book with beautiful colors. It had yellow and orange ellipses on a blue background, and I bought it immediately. It turned out to be about Le Corbusier, whose work was a discovery for me. I saw images of the concrete stairways in the Unité d'Habitation, and I said to myself, 'what an extraordinary sense of form'. The point of the book was to show the artistic aspects of the architect's work. As a result of buying it, I transferred to architecture school."[1]

Born near Valencia in 1951, Calatrava went to primary and secondary school there. Beginning in 1959, he also attended the Arts and Crafts School, Valencia, where he started formal training in drawing and painting. When he was 13, his family took advantage of the recent opening of the borders of Franco's Spain, and sent him to France as an exchange student. After graduating from high school in Valencia, he went to Paris to attend the École des Beaux-Arts, but he arrived in 1968, in the midst of the student uprising. He returned to Valencia and, seduced by a small colorful book, enrolled in the Escuela Tècnica Superior de Arquitectura, where he got a degree in architecture and did postgraduate work in urbanism.

Where others might have ended their studies, Calatrava decided to continue. Attracted by the mathematical rigor that he perceived in certain works of historic architecture, and feeling that his training in Valencia had given him no clear direction, he decided to begin postgraduate studies in civil engineering and enrolled in 1975 at the ETH (Federal Institute of Technology) in Zurich. He received his Ph.D. in 1979. This decision certainly changed his life in many ways. It was during this period that he met and married his wife, Robertina Marangoni, who was a law student in Zurich. Professionally speaking, the keys to Santiago Calatrava's current activity are also to be found in Zurich. As he says, "The desire to start over from zero was extremely strong for me. I was determined to set aside all of what I worked with in architecture school and to learn to draw like an engineer and to think like one, too. I was fascinated by the concept of gravity and resolute in feeling that it was necessary to work with simple forms. I could say that my taste for simplicity in engineering comes in part from my observation of the work of the Swiss engineer Robert Maillart. With simple forms he showed that it is possible to create a strong content and to elicit an emotional response. With the proper combination of force and mass, you can create emotion."

Architect, Engineer, Artist

Calatrava's early interest in art, and the aesthetic sense that drew him to the small book on Le Corbusier, would remain another constant factor in his work, and one of the things that sets him apart in the world of contemporary architecture. Referring to a 2005 exhibition of his art and architecture held at New York's Metropolitan Museum of Art, Calatrava says, "I think that the curator in charge, Gary Tinterow, understood my way of working, because he titled the show 'Sculpture into Architecture' rather than the

1 Interview with Santiago Calatrava, Zurich, February 22, 2006.

Mother and Child, gold-plated brass, black granite, 1990

reverse. Architecture critics haven't gotten over being perplexed by my work." Indeed, while noting that the last time the Metropolitan showed the work of a living architect was in 1973, Nicolai Ouroussoff, when reviewing this show, wrote in *The New York Times*, "No one would argue that Mr. Calatrava's sculptures would make it into the Met on their own merits; as art, they are mostly derivative of the works of dead masters like Brancusi." Going on to a rather brutal conclusion, "One wishes he had left the sculpture back in his studio."[2] This comment above all seems to show a lack of under-standing of Calatrava's sculpture. "In sculpture," he says, "I have used spheres, and cubes, simple forms often related to my knowledge of engineering. It is a sculpture that gave rise to the Turning Torso (Malmö, Sweden, 1999–2004). I must admit that I greatly admire the liberty of a Frank Gehry, or Frank Stella as a sculptor. There is a joy and a liberty in Stella's work that is not present in my sculpture, which is always based in the rough business of mathematics."[3] Calatrava is quite clear about saying that he has always disliked the art gallery circuit, almost never showing his sculpture. He also underlines the fact that "the reaction I receive from artists is very positive. Art is much freer than architecture, because, as Picasso said, some artists work with marble and others with shit." This is not to say that Santiago Calatrava is at all naive about the difficulty of his task. In 1997, he wrote, "Architecture and sculpture are two rivers in which the same water flows. Imagine that sculpture is unfettered plasticity, while architecture is plasticity that must submit to function, and to the obvious notion of

2   Nicolai Ouroussoff, "Buildings Shown as Art and Art as Buildings," *The New York Times*, October 25, 2005.
3   Interview with Santiago Calatrava, Zurich, February 22, 2006.

Emergency Services Center and Pfalzkeller Gallery, St. Gallen, Switzerland, 1988–1998

4 *Julio González Dessiner dans l'espace*, Skira, Kunstmuseum Bern, 1997.

5 Auguste Rodin, *Les Cathédrales de France*, Armand Colin, Paris, 1914.

6 Le Corbusier, *Vers une architecture*, Paris, 1923.

7 Auguste Rodin, *Les Cathédrales*, op cit. "Il n'atteint à la grande expression qu'en donnant toute son etude aux jeux harmoniques de la lumière et de l'ombre, exactement comme fait l'architecte."

human scale (through function). Where sculpture ignores function, unbowed by mundane questions of use, it is superior to architecture as pure expression. But through its rapport with human scale and the environment, through its penetrability and interiority, architecture dominates sculpture in these specific areas."[4]

Calatrava goes so far as to suggest that art must be considered as a source of ideas for architecture. "Why do I make drawings of the human figure? The artist or the architect can send his message across time by the very force of form and shadow. Rodin wrote, 'Harmony in living bodies is the result of the counterbalancing of masses that move; the Cathedral is built on the example of the living body.'[5] Let me give you an example of the importance of art for 20th-century architecture. When Le Corbusier wrote 'Architecture is the masterly, correct, and magnificent play of masses brought together in light' in 1923,[6] how many people knew that he was borrowing from the thought of the sculptor Auguste Rodin? In 1914, in his book *Les Cathédrales de France*, Rodin wrote, 'The sculptor attains great expression only when he gives all his attention to the harmonic play of light and shadow, just as the architect does.'[7] The fact that one of the most famous phrases of modern architecture was inspired not by an architect but by a sculptor underlines the significance of art."

Aside from his consistent interest in art, Santiago Calatrava has also brought a related passion to his own very personal definition of architecture—that of movement: implied but also real, that is to say physical motion. From the early folding doors of his

Musical Star, gold-plated brass, string and black granite, 1999

Ernsting's Warehouse (Coesfeld-Lette, Germany, 1983–1985) to the more recent 115-ton Burke Brise Soleil (Milwaukee Art Museum, Milwaukee, Wisconsin, 1994–2001), he has come back again and again, in his sculpture and in his architecture, to the unusual concept of repetitive, physical movement. Why? "There is a cinematic element in 20th-century art," replies Calatrava. "Artists like Alexander Calder, Naum Gabo, or Moholy-Nagy created sculptures that move. I love their work and it gives me a great emotion. My doctoral thesis 'On the Foldability of Frames' had to do with the fact that a geometric figure can be reduced from three dimensions to two and ultimately to just one. Take a polyhedron and collapse it, making it into a planar surface. Another transformation reduces it to a single line, a single dimension. You can view this as a problem of mathematics or topology. All the mystery of the omnipresent Platonic solids is summed up in the polyhedron. After thinking about these questions, I looked at ancient sculpture in a different light. Works such as the *Discobolus* by Myron create a tension based on an instant of movement, and that is how I became interested in the problem of time, time as a variable. Einstein said, 'God does not play dice with the Universe,' and so it became apparent to me that everything is related to mathematics and the unique dimension of time. Then I thought about statics (the branch of physics concerned with physical systems in static equilibrium) and realized that there is nothing static about them. Everything is potential movement. Newton's second law of motion states that the acceleration of an object is dependent upon two variables: the

Sundial Bridge, Redding, California, 1995–2004

net force acting upon the object and the mass of the object. Mass and acceleration are related, and thus there is time in force. I realized that architecture is full of things that move, from doors to furniture. Architecture itself moves and with a little luck becomes a beautiful ruin. Everything changes, everything dies, and there is an existential meaning in cyclical movements. I wanted to make a door of my own, one that would have a poetic meaning and transform itself into a figure in space, and that is how the Ernsting's project came about."

The Essence of Architecture

The fact that some are uncomfortable with the multiple forms of expression chosen by Santiago Calatrava is probably the best indication that he is on to something important. Today, he is carrying forward one of the most complex and politically sensitive projects imaginable in the United States, the World Trade Center Transportation Hub in the midst of the desolation that New Yorkers have come to call Ground Zero. "We think he is the Da Vinci of our time," said Joseph Seymour, the former executive director of the Port Authority of New York and New Jersey, which is building the station. "He combines light and air and structural elegance with strength." Such praise is not rare, even in the closed world of architecture. In 2005, Santiago Calatrava became the second Spaniard (after Josep Lluís Sert in 1981) to win the prestigious American Institute of Architects' Gold Medal. The AIA Committee on

Design declared, "Santiago Calatrava's work seeks out the essence of architecture. His architecture expands the vision and expresses the energy of the human spirit, captivating the imagination and delighting us in the wonders of what sculptural form and dynamic structure can accomplish. Santiago Calatrava defines the reason for the Gold Medal. His vision elevates the human spirit through the creation of environments in which we live, play, and work."

Santiago Calatrava does not seem to be perturbed by the coexistence of art, architecture, and engineering in his own thought. And yet, with his combined interests, Calatrava is indeed close to the heart of one of the most intense debates in the recent history of construction and design. As Sigfried Giedion wrote in his seminal book *Space, Time and Architecture*, "The advent of the structural engineer with speedier, industrialized form-giving components broke up the artistic bombast and shattered the privileged position of the architect and provided the basis for present-day developments. The 19th-century engineer unconsciously assumed the role of guardian of the new elements he was continually delivering to the architects. He was developing forms that were both anonymous and universal." Giedion retraces the debate about the role of engineering by citing a number of essential dates and events. Amongst them, "1877: In this year the question entered the Académie, when a prize was offered for the best paper discussing 'the union or the separation of engineer and architect.' Davioud, one of the architects of the Trocadéro, won the prize with this answer: 'The accord will never become real, complete, and fruitful until the day that the engineer, the artist, and the scientist are fused together in the same person. We have for a long time lived under the foolish persuasion that art is a kind of activity distinct from all other forms of human intelligence, having its sole source and origin in the personality of the artist himself and in his capricious fancy.'"[8] Though neither Giedion's insistence on the "anonymity" of the work of the engineer, nor Davioud's reference to the "capricious fancy" of the artist seem to fit well with Calatrava's powerful originality, he does appear to meet the Frenchman's requirements for an accord between art, engineering, and architecture. Then, too, Joseph Seymour's reference to the "Da Vinci of our time" also comes to mind.

The catalogue of Santiago Calatrava's 1993 exhibition at the Museum of Modern Art in New York underlines the close relationship of his work to that of other ground-breaking engineers: "Calatrava is part of the distinguished heritage of 20th-century engineering. Like those of the preceding generations—Robert Maillart, Pier Luigi Nervi, Eduardo Torroja, and Felix Candela—Calatrava goes beyond an approach that merely solves technical problems. Structure, for these engineers, is a balance between the scientific criterion of efficiency and the innovation of new forms. Calatrava considers engineering 'the art of the possible,' and seeks a new vocabulary of form that is based on technical know-how, yet is not an anthem to techniques."[9] The first figure cited, Robert Maillart (1872–1940), graduated from the ETH in Zurich in 1894 and went on to create some of the most spectacular modern bridges, and to make innovative use of concrete. His Giesshübel Warehouse in Zurich (1910) employed a concrete slab "mushroom ceiling" for the first time, permitting Maillart to do away with the use of beams. As Matilda McQuaid writes, "Maillart was one of the first engineers of this century to break completely from masonry construction and apply a technically appropriate and elegant solution to reinforced concrete construction. Although the technical idea in Calatrava's work is neither the primary motivation, as

Temporary Swimming Pool, ETH Zurich, 1979

8 Sigfried Giedion, *Space, Time and Architecture*, 5th edition, Harvard University Press, Cambridge, Massachusetts, 1976.
9 Matilda McQuaid, *Santiago Calatrava, Structure and Expression*, The Museum of Modern Art, New York, 1993.

Acleta Alpine Motor Bridge, Disentis, Switzerland.
One of a series of 1979 studies carried out by
Calatrava at the ETH, Zurich

with Maillart, nor understated, it informs the overall expression of the structure. His work becomes an 'intertwinement of plastic expression and structural revelation, producing results that possibly can be best described as a synthesis of aesthetics and structural physics.'"[10]

Although he naturally admires the work of Maillart, Santiago Calatrava is quick to point out that his bridges are very different from those of his predecessor, if only because of their siting. "Maillart's bridges," says Calatrava, "are often set in beautiful mountain scenery. His achievement was to introduce successfully an artificial element into such magnificent locations." "Today," he continues, "I believe that one of the most

10 Ibid.

Puerto Bridge, Ondarroa, Spain, 1989–1995

important tasks is to reconsider the periphery of cities. Most often public works in such areas are purely functional, and yet even near railroad tracks, or spanning polluted rivers, bridges can have a remarkably positive effect. By creating an appropriate environment, they can have a symbolic impact whose ramifications go far beyond their immediate location."[11]

Calatrava's work has undoubtedly been influenced by that of Felix Candela, who was born in Madrid in 1910, and emigrated to Mexico in 1939, where he created a number of remarkable thin-shelled concrete structures, such as the Iglesia de la Virgen Milagrosa (Navarte, Mexico, 1955), a design entirely based on hyperbolic parabaloids. Another Spaniard, the Madrid engineer Eduardo Torroja (1899–1961), was fascinated by the use of organic or vegetal forms, whose undeniable sculptural presence may well spring from the influence of Gaudí. Many of Santiago Calatrava's references are to Spanish, and more specifically Catalan, architects or artists. "What fascinates me in the personality of Goya, for example," says Calatrava, "is that he is one of the first artists to renounce the idea, as Rembrandt had before him, of serving any one master. What I admire in Miró's work," he continues, "is its remarkable silence, as well as his radical rejection of everything conventional." Although Gaudí provides him with an example like that of Maillart, Calatrava seems more at ease speaking about the sculptor Julio González. "The father and grandfather of González were metalworkers for Gaudí on projects like the Güell Park. Then they went to Paris, and that is where Julio González's metal works derive from. With all due modesty," concludes Calatrava, "one might say that what we do is a natural continuation of the work of Gaudí and of González, a work of artisans moving toward abstract art."[12]

The kind of art that Santiago Calatrava is referring to is apparent in his most successful bridges and buildings, and yet it remains difficult to describe in words.

11 Interview with Santiago Calatrava, Zurich, June 1997.
12 Ibid.

Another of the essential figures of 20th-century engineering, the Italian Pier Luigi Nervi, attempted such a definition in a series of lectures he delivered at Harvard in 1961: "It is very difficult to explain the reason for our immediate approval of forms which come to us from a physical world with which we, seemingly, have no direct tie whatsoever. Why do these forms satisfy and move us in the same manner as natural things such as flowers, plants, and landscapes to which we have become accustomed through numberless generations? It can also be noted that these achievements have in common a structural essence, a necessary absence of all decoration, a purity of line and shape more than sufficient to define an authentic style, a style I have termed the *truthful style*. I realize how difficult it is to find the right words to express this concept. When I make these remarks to friends, I am often told that this view of the near future is terribly sad, that perhaps it would be better to renounce voluntarily the further tightening of the bonds between our creations and the physical laws, if indeed these ties must lead us to a fatal monotony. I do not find this pessimism justified. Binding as technical demands may be, there always remains a margin of freedom sufficient to show the personality of the creator of a work and, if he be an artist, to allow that his creation, even in its strict technical obedience, become a real and true work of art."[13]

13 Pier Luigi Nervi, *Aesthetics and Technology in Building, The Charles Eliot Norton Lectures, 1961–1962*, Harvard University Press, Cambridge, Massachusetts, 1965.

Wings and a Prayer

Calatrava's sensitivity to urban design is undoubtedly what won him the competitions in Lisbon, but also in Liège, or more recently in Manhattan for the symbolically charged

Bach de Roda–Felipe II Bridge, Barcelona, Spain, 1984–1987

World Trade Center Transportation Hub. He seems genuinely to feel that the architect can elevate a place such as a railway station and give it a sense of the sacred. When asked if his idea is to make spaces that are comfortable and humane or rather to reach for something more, his answer reveals much about his creative process. "Everything is based on man," he says, "but in man's complexity, the sacred exists, or there wouldn't be so many people crowding into the Pantheon in Rome to see the round hole in the dome. What about railway stations? If you take the example of the modern stations in Switzerland—in Zurich or Basel, for example—you get the feeling that you are in a shopping mall. Grand Central Terminal in New York seems to come from a different planet. By exalting abstract values, architecture is capable of being a catalyst for enormous events. But if you go at it with a purely functionalist attitude, you don't catalyze anything. You wind up with a mediocre shopping mall. The feeling that I get in the Central Hall of Grand Central Terminal is the product of great intelligence. It gives a particular sense, even a sacred aspect to commerce. While sacrificing nothing of its utility, the station becomes an act of celebration. Look at all that has sprung up around the void at the heart of Grand Central—the Seagram Building and Park Avenue itself. In America, no building resembles the Pantheon so closely in these terms. Look at what the architects have placed in the center of the great hall—a clock and a small

stand intended to give away timetables—two elements intended to give, rather than to take, from travelers. We need beauty and beauty can generate great things."[14]

When describing his plans for the new World Trade Center Transportation Hub, Calatrava lists his materials as "glass, steel, concrete, stone, and light." The architect has understood that light must shine into the very heart of one of the darkest events in recent American history, and that he has touched the sensitivity of New Yorkers even before the wings of his new station rise up out of the ground. Although suggestive of motifs from many traditions (the Byzantine mandorla, the wings of cherubim above the Ark of the Covenant, the sheltering wings on Egyptian canopic urns), the form of his glass roof is summed up, according to Santiago Calatrava, by the image of a bird released from a child's hands. Whatever its symbolism, the $2 billion complex will also address the overly complex layering of lower Manhattan's transport system, born of a century of progressive extensions, enlargements, and changes of direction. Both echoing Santiago Calatrava's own feelings about the importance of an uplifting design, Michael Bloomberg, the Mayor of New York, declared, "Today we unveil the design of downtown's new PATH station and we imagine that future generations will look at this building as a true record of our lives today as we rebuild our city. What will they see in Santiago Calatrava's thrilling work? They'll see creativity in design, and strength in

Lyon-Saint Exupéry Airport Railway Station, Satolas, France, 1989–1994

14 Interview with Santiago Calatrava, Zurich, February 22, 2006.

A model of the future World Trade Center Transportation Hub, New York, New York, 2003–2009

construction... And they'll see optimism—a building appearing to take flight—just like the neighborhood it serves."

The Vertical Challenge

From the largely horizontal world of bridges that he masters so well, Calatrava has ventured boldly into the verticality of towers on numerous occasions in his career, though he now seems to be concentrating even more on such design. Most recently, Calatrava has designed three very different towers, the Turning Torso, based on his drawings of a male torso; the 80 South Street Tower in New York, made of 12 canti-levered, glazed cubes inspired by a series of sculptures he made up to 20 years earlier; and, most surprisingly, the Chicago Spire, a 160-story, 610-meter-high tower that will become the tallest building in the United States. In each instance, the architect shows that he in no way feels that towers are outdated as symbols, or as functional, efficient forms of design. Both the Turning Torso and the 80 South Street Tower embody his idea of using the science of statics to give the impression of the movement inherent in the concept of mass. Based on mathematical calculations, these works escape the realm of dry science to evoke the body or the uplifting sentiment that only a great building can inspire.

The New York Times prompted Brancusi to describe Calatrava's sculptures, in itself not a disparaging comparison, and yet it may be true that the architect-engineer seems to call on examples from the early part of the 20th century more readily than recent thinking and art. Calatrava quotes Einstein, who famously said, "God does not play dice with the Universe." But at the time, the master of modern physics was reacting to the advances of the Quantum Theory, and in particular Werner Heisenberg's Uncer-tainty Principle, which stated, with reference to subatomic particles, that, "The more precisely the position is determined, the less precisely the momentum is known in this instant, and vice versa." Although many artists and architects since then (1927) have embodied the reasoning of uncertain times in their work, why is it that Calatrava seems

Turning Torso, Thassos marble, chrome-plated steel, string, 1991

so firmly anchored in another era—one where Platonic solids might have ruled rather than the complexity described by the theories of Benoît Mandelbrot, for example. "In the 1980s," says Calatrava, "there was indeed experimentation in architecture that had to do with the Chaos Theory and the sort of mathematics used to predict the movement of a stock exchange or the weather. But there is a programmatic element in Einstein's famous sentence that I would like to underline. Order exists, and I am tempted to say that we have already gone beyond the Chaos Theory and begun to think of the order of design. Personally, I have never wanted to render anything explicit in architecture other than order. I have indeed always referred to pure geometry and to controlled movement. The only time chance may enter into my work is when I make a sketch. Where current architecture is concerned, I note that those who choose models based on uncertainty, in the form of disorder or deconstruction, if you will, must refer strongly to engineering when they seek to give some maturity to their work. People like Daniel Libeskind proudly refer to their past experience with mathematics, and it is obvious that the science of engineers is essential to their architecture. I might be so bold as to say that I have always played the game from the center."[15]

A Collection of Pearls

At the age of 55, it is clear that Santiago Calatrava is entering the mature phase of his career, and, as his recent works testify, he has no intention of becoming duller as time goes by. It is easy to see where Calatrava has been, but not as obvious to tell where he will go in the future. This very point may well be a key to understanding his thought. "Imagine that you don't know where you are going," he says. "The baggage you bring with you is what you carry inside. For me, this is almost a situation of paranoia, or of schizophrenia. I have a sense of forms born of 14 years of university studies—I have encountered mathematics, which I love. When I look at the work of Picasso, Cézanne, or Matisse, all of which moves me, I must notice that they never engaged in abstraction, except in limited details of their works. They worked to create an emotion and I am also born of their universe. I have long been inspired by a simple phrase of Michelangelo, 'l'architettura dipende dalle membra dell'uomo.' To use the human body as a means of expression is and will remain important."

No matter how significant mathematics and the science of engineering are in the work of Santiago Calatrava, it is art and emotion that drive him to create works that far surpass the mundane calculation of forces. "Life is like a collection of pearls," says Calatrava. "You find one here and another there on your road. What is the sense of function in architecture? It is love, the love that one gives others, the generosity of the architect. There is a great secret in architecture and that is its philanthropic nature, and that philanthropy can be understood in the terms of function. A building functions well out of love for human beings. The secret of philanthropy in architecture is in its function. Beauty is given through intelligence or intuition. In architecture, it is necessary to draw every detail. Each act, except the emotion that sets you on your way, is an act of intelligence. Architecture is what makes beautiful ruins; it is the most abstract of all the arts."[16]

The New York Times Capsule, New York, 2001

15 Interview with Santiago Calatrava, Zurich, February 22, 2006.
16 Ibid.

The figure studies of Calatrava are not necessarily related directly to specific works. This watercolor, however, does show the spirit that inhabits much of his architecture.

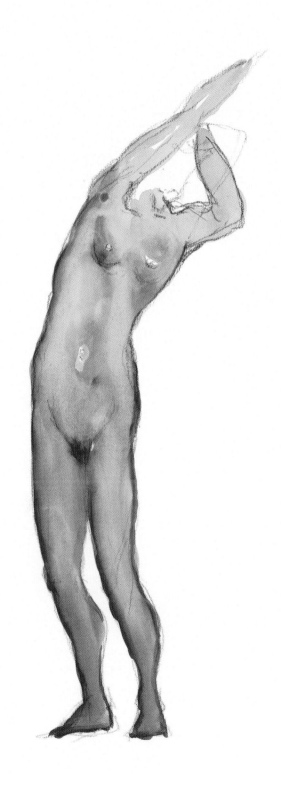

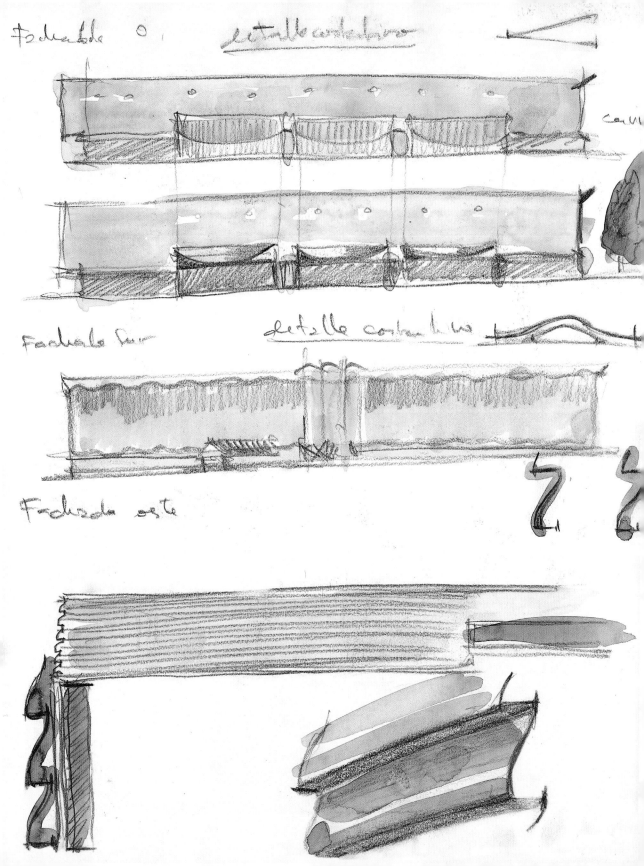

1983–1985 ▸ Ernsting's Warehouse
Coesfeld-Lette, Germany

Opposite page: Sketches by Calatrava show the doors in open and closed positions as well as the opposite facade of the structure.

Right: The warehouse with its bay doors in the open position

Below: The bay doors closing

Ernsting's is a well-known German clothing manufacturer. At the company's Coesfeld-Lette campus, the warehouse that Calatrava built in the 1980s is now located opposite David Chipperfield's Service Center (1998–2001), an elegant minimalist design surrounded by a garden conceived by the noted Belgian landscape architects Jacques and Peter Wirtz. Calatrava worked with an initial warehouse form proposed by Gerzi, a specialist in facilities for the textile industry. He decided to cover the Gerzi structure with untreated aluminum, a typical industrial material, seeking to make each façade different while maintaining the overall unity imposed by the cladding. The aluminum is treated according to light patterns, corrugated on the south where it "responds to sunlight as if it were a giant sculpture," or with a specially formed S-profile on the north, where the façade receives only midday sun. The most surprising feature suggested by Calatrava is to be found in the form of the three large loading bay doors, measuring 13x5 meters. The hinged aluminum ribs rise to form a concave arch as they open, creating canopies. A sculpture by Calatrava with a "form based on the human eye" was part of the design process. "Here," says the architect, "the form became an experiment in kinetics, used to investigate the mechanical transformation of planes in a building."

1983–1990 ▸ Stadelhofen Station
Zurich, Switzerland

Opposite page: The curved train platforms and Calatrava's canopies

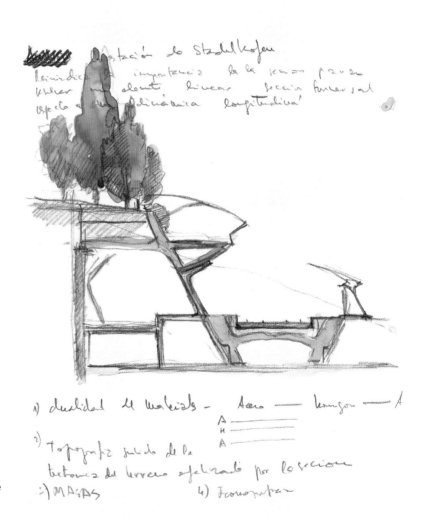

Calatrava's sketch—corresponding to the left side of the image on the opposite page—shows how the station is embedded into the hillside.

For this expansion and redefinition of an existing station, intended as an inner-city node for a rapid transit system, Santiago Calatrava participated in the competition with the architect Arnold Amsler and the landscape architect Werner Rüeger. Adjacent to a curved, green embankment near the Bellevueplatz and not far from the Theaterstrasse, the Stadelhofen Railway Station reveals its structure only as the traveler reaches the train tracks. A transparent glass canopy covers the entire length of the platform, giving it a great deal of natural light in spite of the fairly enclosed site. By proposing to undercut and redefine the existing hillside while maintaining its slope, the architects

Calatrava is careful to bring natural light into the underground spaces, rendering the concrete surfaces less harsh.

The underground passageway in the station retains something of the zoomorphic forms frequently used by the architect.

obviated the need for a tunnel. A cable trellis creates a "transparent green canopy that softens the station's intrusion into its environment." Below ground, a parallel shopping area follows the curve of the tracks themselves. Mouthlike hatches or doorways intended to permit the evening closure of the facility lead downwards toward this commercial zone.

1984–1987·Bach de Roda–Felipe II Bridge
Barcelona, Spain

Opposite page: Lit at night, the bridge becomes a symbol of renewal in an otherwise rather rundown area of the city.

Right: Although the upper, more visible parts of the bridge give an impression of lightness, the massive concrete anchors incarnate the necessary solidity of the structure.

Above: A sketch by Calatrava of a human figure is not the specific inspiration for this bridge, but rather an evocation of forms and forces.

With its overall length of 128 meters and its twin inclined and split arches, this bridge was one of the first to contribute to the reputation of Santiago Calatrava. Indeed, the 60-degree inclination of the lateral steel arches appears almost like a stylistic signature of the architect-engineer. Crossing a kind of no-man's-land originally created by the existence of railway lines, the bridge links the Bach de Roda and Felipe II streets, reconnecting a large section of the city to the sea. Combining powerful concrete supports, monolithic granite columns, and a steel arch structure that becomes progressively lighter as it rises, the Bach de Roda–Felipe II Bridge also demonstrates Calatrava's adherence to a hierarchy of materials and forms, chosen in relation to their distance from the ground.

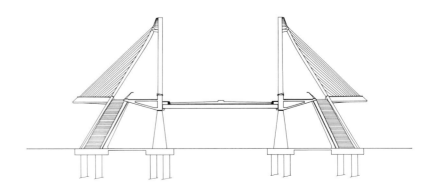

Right: A schematic elevation shows the double, symmetric design of the bridge.

1987–1992 ▸ Alamillo Bridge and La Cartuja Viaduct

Seville, Spain

Opposite page: The dynamic form of the bridge, all the more spectacular at night, is in part due to the lack of backstays.

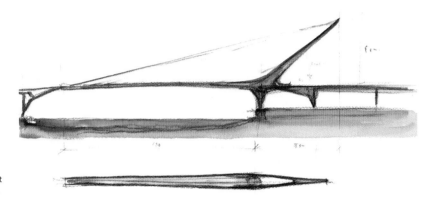

Right: Calatrava's apparently simple sketch in fact demonstrates his knowledge of both architecture and engineering.

Above: Another figure sketch by the architect shows his interest in stretching positions and physical tension.

Part of a plan initiated by the government of the region of Andalusia on the occasion of Expo '92, this bridge has a 200-meter span over the Meandro San Jeronimo, a shallow branch of the Guadalquivir River. Its most striking feature is a 142-meter-high pylon, inclined at an angle of 58 degrees, the same as that of the Pyramid of Cheops. Filled with cement, this tower is sufficiently massive to counterbalance the bridge deck, obviating the need for backstays, and allowing the bridge to be held up with just 13 pairs of cables. Santiago Calatrava's personal research on the Alamillo Bridge involved a 1986 sculpture called *Running Torso* made of cubes of marble held in equilibrium at an angle by a wire under tension. His drawings of running figures also come to mind. He originally proposed a second bridge, located 1.5 kilometers from the first one, with a mirror image pylon at the point where the road crosses the same river again, but the client opted instead for the 526-meter-long Puente de La Cartuja Viaduct, with its two 10-meter-wide lanes, which was used as the northern entrance to the Expo '92 site. The double bridge concept would have created an enormous, partially imaginary triangle, with its point high in the sky above the Expo site. Frequently imitated by other engineers and architects, the inclined pylon of the Alamillo Bridge stands out as a symbol of modern Seville.

1989–1992 ▸ Montjuic Communications Tower
Barcelona, Spain

Opposite page: The unexpected form of the tower can be seen as an evocation of Olympic sports, such as javelin throwing.

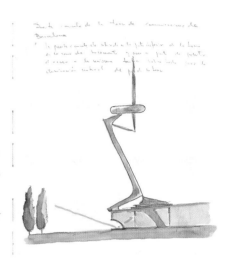

Right: Calatrava's sketch and related commentary show his method in conceiving the tower, not only from an aesthetic point of view, but also from an engineer's perspective.

Above: Renewing his interest in movable elements in architecture, Calatrava included an eye-shaped opening in the base of the tower.

Located near the Palau Sant Jordi designed by the Japanese architect Arata Isozaki, the Montjuic Communications Tower is 136 meters high. Built like its neighbor for the 1992 Olympic Games, it is based on an inclined trunk with an annular element containing the actual antennas above. The base, closed by a door formed by metal blades, is related to his studies of the human eye. This door was developed along similar lines to the loading bay doors of the Ernsting's Warehouse in Coesfeld-Lette, Germany. Acting like a sundial, the trunk projects a shadow onto the circular platform. The platform at the base, a brick drum containing the communications equipment installed at the time of its competition, is covered in broken tiles, evoking the Güell Park by Antoni Gaudí. Related to both the geographic and solar locations of the site, the Montjuic Tower is at once a symbol of the Olympic Games and of the progressive, artistically oriented history of Barcelona itself. Calatrava's sense of drama and suspended equilibrium is just as evident in this tower as it is in any of his bridges. The structure is by no means anthropomorphic, but it is sufficiently related to the body and its movement to elicit in visitors a feeling of familiarity.

1989–1994·Lyon-Saint Exupéry Airway Railway Station

Satolas, France

Opposite page: An interior view of the station hall uses the design of the overhead skylights to evoke a strong image of flight.

Right: Seen in profile, the structure brings to mind a landing bird, perhaps even a prehistoric creature.

Originally called the Lyon Satolas Station, this project is surely one of Calatrava's best-known works. The architect was the winner of a competition organized by the Rhône-Alpes Region and the Lyon Chamber of Commerce and Industry (CCIL). The competition brief called for a building that would provide smooth passenger flow while creating an exciting and symbolic "gateway to the region." The shape of this 5,600-square-meter facility, which was designed for the French national railway company (SNCF) to connect the high-speed train network (TGV) to the Lyon Airport in Satolas, is more closely related to Calatrava's sculptures than to any animal. Built at a total cost of 600 million francs in three phases, the station accommodates six tracks, with the middle two encased in a concrete shell for trains that pass through at high speeds (300 km/h). A 180-meter-long steel connecting bridge linking the facility to the airport terminal gives the plan a shape that might bring to mind a stingray as much as a bird. Its essential feature remains the main hall with its 1,300-ton roof, measuring 120 x 100 meters, and a maximum height of 40 meters and a span of 53 meters.

Below: A photo of the station seen in the evening from the front emphasizes the strong upward movement of the two "wings."

Bottom: Calatrava's sketches are almost identical to the actual building in terms of both form and engineering.

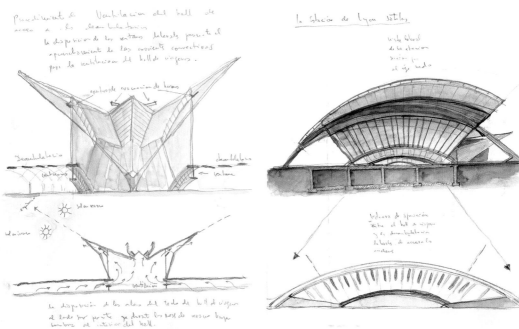

Right: The dynamic shape of the skylights animates the interior space of the station with changing exterior light conditions.

Right: As is frequently the case, Calatrava's successive concrete supports recall bone structures, such as a rib cage.

1990–2000 ▸ Sondica Airport and Control Tower
Bilbao, Spain

Opposite page: Where airport control towers are usually static in appearance, Calatrava's design imparts a sense of movement.

Right: The airport terminal also evokes movement; in this case, the upward lift of takeoff.

Below: A section of the control tower showing the internal spiral stair

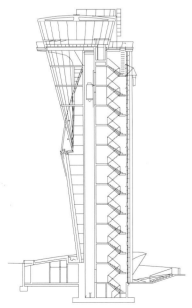

After having been asked in 1990 to design a new four-gate airport facility for the Basque city of Bilbao, Santiago Calatrava was commissioned four years later to double the size of the terminal, located 10 kilometers north of the city. The architect responded with a triangular plan, amply glazed structure whose roof sweeps upward in the direction of the landing field. Where glass is not used, the concrete structure is treated with a unifying aluminum cladding. Departures are located on the upper floor, and arrivals below. Able to handle two million passengers a year as of 2000, Sondica Airport was conceived eventually to receive up to five times more travelers. Santiago Calatrava's design for the new Bilbao Airport facilities included the construction of a 42-meter-high control tower, located 270 meters from the terminal building (1993–1996). Inverting the normal typology for such structures, the tower is designed to have a progressively larger volume as it rises, culminating in a control deck affording 360-degree visibility. Built of reinforced concrete with some aluminum cladding, the tower has become the symbol of the airport itself.

Above: The interior of the terminal calls not only the metaphor of wings, but also undoubtedly on that of human eyes.

Left: Calatrava's knowledge of engineering permits him to make great volumes appear to float on delicate bases.

Above: Though the rhythm of the architect's earlier stations is brought to mind in the terminal, he appears to have simplified his zoomorphic impulse, or perhaps rendered it more abstract.

Right: A simplified elevation sketch evokes the imagery of flight.

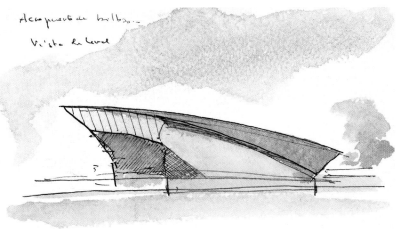

1991–2003 ▸ Tenerife Auditorium
Santa Cruz de Tenerife, Canary Islands, Spain

pposite page: The solar, or perhaps ocular,
esign of the auditorium roof resolves problems
f acoustics and lighting even as it tends toward a
ore spiritual dimension.

ight: Calatrava is a master of watercolor sketches
at capture the fundamental forces and shapes
f his designs.

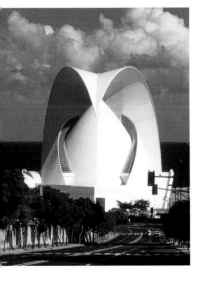

bove: The completed structure seen from the
ront takes on a sculptural shape that sets
Calatrava apart from his contemporaries.

Completed in 2003, this 1,558-seat concert hall is located at the intersection of the Tres
de Mayo Avenue and Maritima Avenue in the city of Santa Cruz de Tenerife. The facility
also includes a chamber music hall with seating for 428. On this site in the harbor, the
city expressed "a desire for a dynamic, monumental building that would not only be a
place for music and culture, but would also create a focal point for the area." With its
distinctive concrete shell roof, in a curved triangular form culminating 60 meters
above the plaza surrounding the building, this concert hall is one of the most visually
spectacular structures designed by Calatrava. Located on a 154×100 meter rectangular
site that has the particularity of including a 60-meter change in levels, the concert hall
is set on a stepped platform or plinth that contains technical facilities and changing
rooms. The roof of the shell of the structure is clad in broken tile, while local volcanic
basalt is used for much of the paving and the cladding of the plinth. A 50-meter-high
dome covers the main hall, recalling a number of Santiago Calatrava's studies of the
human eye and its lid.

Above: Internal spaces take on a sinuous shape that often recall the twisting, stretching forms of Calatrava's figure studies.

Right: White spaces with ample natural light make the interiors change their appearance as the sun moves through the sky.

Far right: Playing on complex curves and unexpected geometric forms, the architect animates his building and frequently creates formal surprises.

Above: The profile of the auditorium seen from across the water forms an iconic presence that dominates its surroundings.

Left: A sketch by the architect shows the auditorium as it is seen from the front.

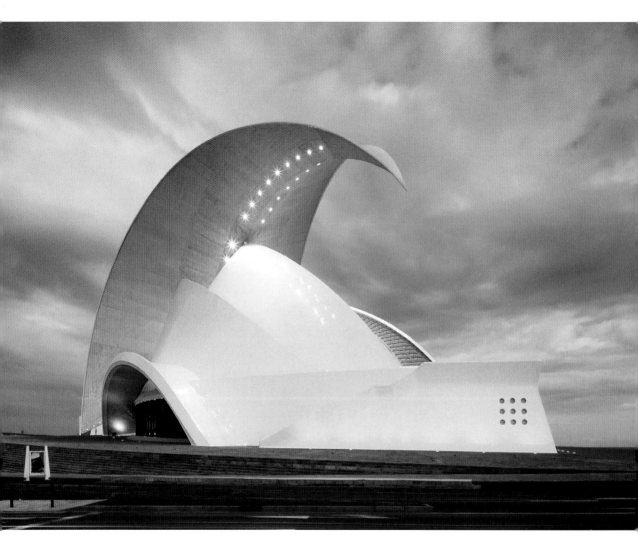

Above: The strange form of the auditorium can neither be accurately described as anthropomorphic nor zoomorphic. It is rather an abstract synthesis of both these and other sources of inspiration.

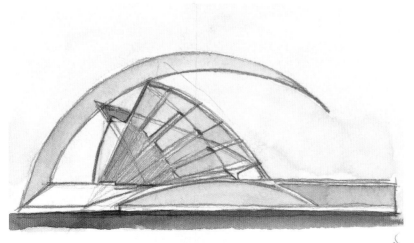

Left: A watercolor sketch simplifies the structure and renders it more sculptural.

Right: An almost surreal balance of form and harmony inhabits this building, perhaps more than any other by Calatrava.

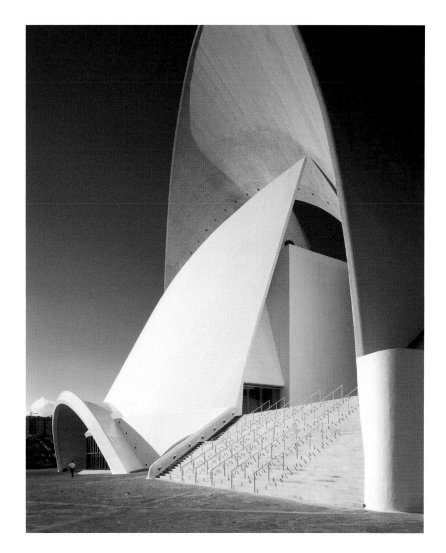

Below: Elements of the building take on unexpected, abstract forms depending on the angle of view and lighting conditions.

Below right: A plan of the auditorium reveals a functional design despite the apparent extravagance of the building's exterior.

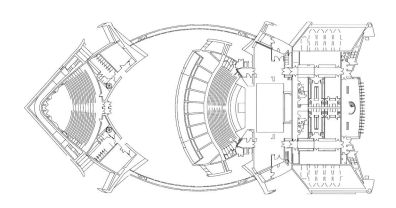

1991–2006 ▸ City of Arts and Sciences / Opera House

Planetarium, Science Museum, and L'Umbracle, 1991–2000;
Opera House, 1996–2006 ▸ Valencia, Spain

Opposite page: The concrete ribs of the Science Museum

Right: The eye-shaped planetarium and IMAX theater with its shade in the open position

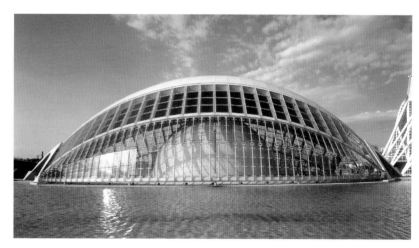

Right: The structure with its folding canopy closed

Part of a long-standing effort on the part of the government of Valencia to rehabilitate a 35-hectare area at the eastern periphery of the city, lodged between a large highway and the Turia River, Calatrava's City of Arts and Sciences took more than 10 years to be completed. The planetarium, an IMAX theater, with its elliptical, or rather eye-shaped, plan and hemispheric dome with movable ribbed covering and an area of almost 2,600 square meters, was built between 1995 and 1998. The 241-meter-long, 41,530-square-meter Príncipe Felipe Science Museum is based on an asymmetrical repetition of tree and riblike forms filled with glass to admit ample daylight. The Opera House completed this ambitious composition.

Conceived as the final element in the City of Arts and Sciences complex, rising to a height of 75 meters on its western edge, the Valencia Opera House was "designed as a

Above: A night view showing the planetarium in the foreground and the Science Museum to the rear

Right: Pages from a sketchbook by the architect show the clear relation of the planetarium to the form of the human eye.

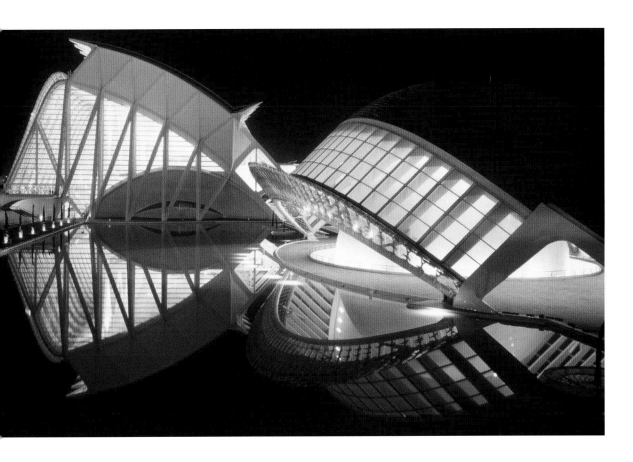

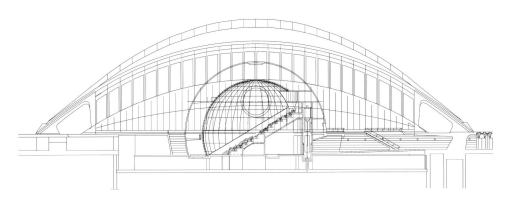

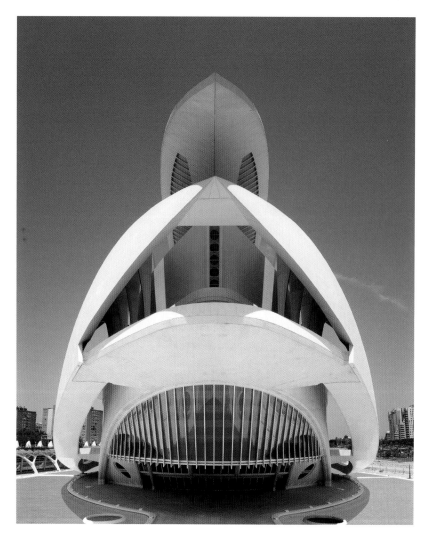

Left: The front of the Valencia Opera House (Palau de les Arts)

Opposite page bottom: The unusual forms used by Calatrava sometimes bring to mind the lyrical compositions of Oscar Niemeyer.

Right: A layering of openings evokes a biological or anthropomorphic inspiration.

Far right: Numerous openings bring ample natural light into the structure.

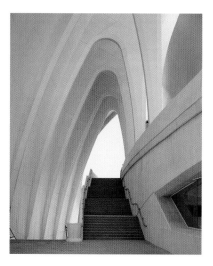

series of apparently random volumes, which become unified through their enclosure within two symmetrical, cut-away concrete shells." Calatrava defines the design as being akin to a "monumental sculpture." The central volume of the complex is occupied by the 1,706-seat auditorium as well as the equipment required for the stage settings. A smaller auditorium, conceived mainly for chamber music, seats 380, while a large auditorium to the east, partially covered by the open shell, can seat 1,520 persons. Located adjacent to the main building is a 400-seat auditorium for experimental theater and dance, with gallery space for art exhibitions.

1993–1998 ▸ Oriente Station
Lisbon, Portugal

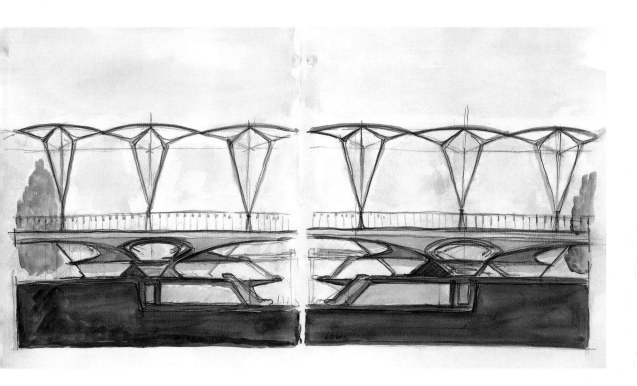

Above: A sketch by Calatrava shows the tree-like shapes of the station platforms sitting above the passageways and entrances of the facility.

Part of an ambitious plan in connection with the Universal Exposition of 1998 that was held in the Portuguese capital, this new train station is located in a former industrial zone about five kilometers from the historic center of Lisbon, not far from the broad Tagus River. The most spectacular aspect of the project is undoubtedly the 78 x 238 meter covering over the eight raised railway tracks whose typology might recall that of a forest. The architect, winner of an invited competition, was obliged to make do with the existing tracks, set up on a nine-meter-high embankment. Rather than emphasizing the break between the city and the river implied by the station, Calatrava has sought, here as elsewhere, to open passageways and reestablish links. Prior to the station's construction, the railway tracks had marked a distinct barrier between the residential and industrial parts of the city. The new complex includes two large glass and steel awnings over the openings, measuring no less than 112 meters in length and 11 meters in width. There is a bus station and car park, a metro station below, and a longitudinal gallery accommodating commercial space included in Calatrava's brief. Ticketing and service facilities are located five meters below the tracks, with an atrium marking the longitudinal gallery five meters lower, and the opening on the river side intended as the main access point, serving the area that has developed subsequent to the 1998 event. As the architect concludes, "Conceived as the Expo's primary transport connection, Oriente Station has proven to be the main component in the trans-

Opposite page: The station platforms provide shelter but also ample contact with the exterior and daylight.

Opposite page top: The lower level of the station with the actual train platforms located above ground level gives a dynamic impression of lightness, emphasized by the angled supports of the structure.

Right: Calatrava's sketch shows the extent to which he has simplified and rendered more abstract the original forest inspiration of the design.

Opposite page bottom: Sketches of a human figure and structural elements show the rather unexpected way in which the architect relates the body to his designs.

Below: A passageway through the station features a high vaulted ceiling, testifying to the architect's frequent use of daylight in such normally dark spaces.

Comparacion destructures mobiles con la naturaleza
ARBOLES   BAUSCHANZLY

magnetz III

formation of the area. It has become one of Europe's most comprehensive transport nodes: an important interchange for high-speed intercity trains, rapid regional transport, standard rail services, and tram and metro networks."

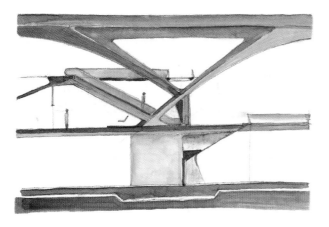

Above: The main entrance canopy and station platforms above seen at night

Left: Calatrava's sketch shows how he plays on his knowledge of statics to give an impression of movement and disequilibrium when in fact all elements are carefully balanced.

Opposite page: This image emphasizes the layering and complexity introduced to the structure by Calatrava. The lower, concrete elements evoke strength and weight, while the upper areas of the building are light and metallic.

1994–1997 · Campo Volantín Footbridge
Bilbao, Spain

Opposite page: The tilting arc of the bridge, combined with its curvature, gives a strong impression of movement or even of apparent disequilibrium.

Right: The bridge links rather gray areas located close to Frank Gehry's Guggenheim Bilbao.

Below: Sketches show the powerful cantilever effect of the approach to the bridge.

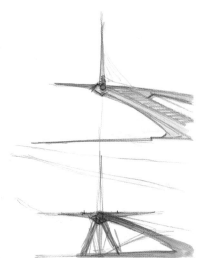

This inclined parabolic arch structure has a total span of 75 meters. Serving to link a rundown commercial area called Uribitarte with the city of Bilbao across the Nervión River, the Campo Volantín Footbridge is one aspect of a vast campaign of urban renewal, which includes Frank Gehry's Guggenheim Bilbao Museum, and Calatrava's own Sondica Airport project. As in many other designs by Santiago Calatrava, an apparent disequilibrium, or rather a sense of frozen movement, is heightened by the lightness of the structure and the steel uprights that run from the arch to the deck of the bridge every 5.7 meters. Its spectacular night lighting and its glass-surfaced deck emphasize the symbolic importance of the bridge, which may indeed have participated in urban renewal. Commissioned by local authorities, the bridge now takes its name not from the Uribitarte area, but from the Campo de Volantín, a street on the opposite bank.

1994–2001 ▸ Milwaukee Art Museum
Milwaukee, Wisconsin, USA

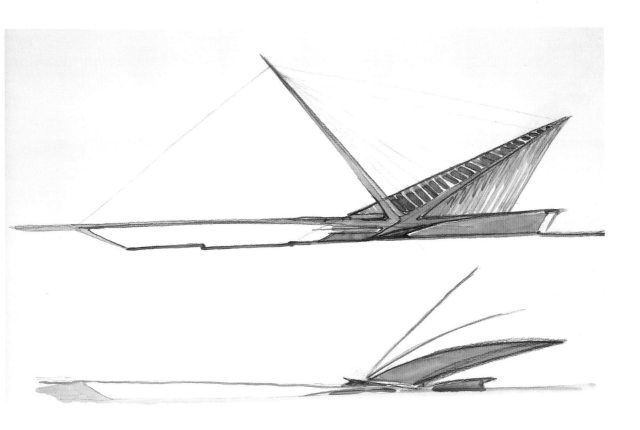

Above: As always fascinated by movement in architecture, Santiago Calatrava imagined a folding *brise soleil* for the Milwaukee Art Museum.

Opposite page: An evening profile of the building emphasizes the complex sequence of balanced elements brought into play by the architect.

The Milwaukee Art Museum was housed in a 1957 structure designed by Eero Saarinen as a War Memorial overlooking Lake Michigan. The architect David Kahler added a large slab structure to the museum in 1975. In 1994, the Trustees of the Milwaukee Art Museum considered a total of 77 architects for a "new grand entrance, a point of orientation for visitors, and a redefinition of the museum's identity through the creation of a strong image." Santiago Calatrava won the competition with his proposal for a 27-meter-high glass and steel reception hall shaded by a movable sunscreen (christened the "Burke Brise Soleil"). Made of steel plates welded and stiffened inside, the 115-ton *brise soleil* consists of two equal wing elements formed by 36 fins whose lengths range between 32 and eight meters. A computerized system automatically overrides the manual control of the structure when wind speed exceeds 40 miles per hour. As the architect explains the overall project, "The design adds 13,200 square meters to the existing 14,900 square meters, including a linear wing (made of glass and stainless steel, with lamella roof) that is set at a right angle to Saarinen's structure. At shore level, the expansion houses: the atrium; 1,500 square meters of gallery space for

Above: The image above shows the extension with its *brise soleil* in the closed position.

Right: Calatrava's sketch showing the wings of the sunshade fully open

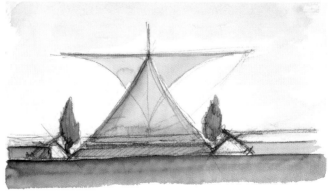

temporary exhibitions; an education center with 300-seat lecture hall; and a gift shop. The 100-seat restaurant, which is placed at the focal point of the pavilion, commands panoramic views onto the lake." Calatrava is also responsible for the Reiman Bridge, a suspended pedestrian link between downtown and the lakefront.

Above: The *brise soleil* in the open position, with the inclined mast of the approach bridge visible to the left

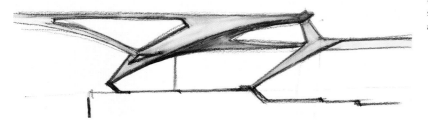

Left: The cantilevered angling of the elements seen in this sketch is typical of Calatrava's approach.

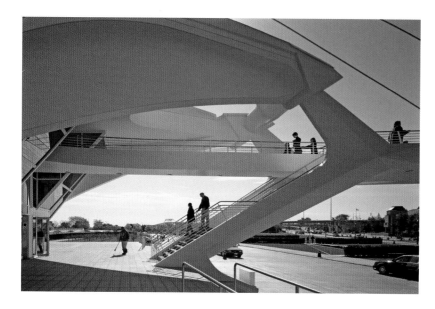

Left: The actual stairs and approach sequence resolved on the basis of the sketch above

Left: Angled, curved arches with ample glazing render this passageway dynamic and inviting.

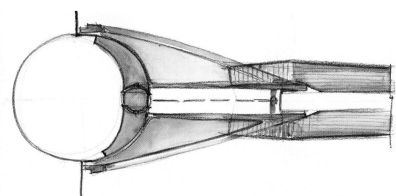

Above: Though the function of this space is purely secular, Calatrava imparts a sense of spirituality to the design.

Left: The eye, whether used in plan or in section, remains a fundamental inspiration for Calatrava, who refers to his own eye in explaining this recurring theme.

1998–2001 ▸ Mujer Bridge
Buenos Aires, Argentina

Beginning in the late 1980s, Buenos Aires began to take an interest in urban planning and development strategies designed to attract international capital, and in particular sought to revitalize the city's rundown port area, the Puerto Madero. Named after the engineer Eduardo Madero, who proposed the construction of the port in 1881, the area was already idle by 1925, when a new port was built to the north. Various proposals, including one by Le Corbusier (1929), sought to revitalize the area, but it was not until 1989 that the Corporación Antiguo Puerto Madero formulated a redevelopment master plan for the 170-hectare site. In this instance, the client asked Calatrava to design a footbridge for Dock 3 in the Puerto Madero, which was insufficiently connected to the city. His solution, the Puente de la Mujer, is "a structure that consists of a rotating suspension bridge, 102 meters long, set between a pair of fixed approach spans. The central section is suspended by cables from an inclined pylon 39 meters high. This section of the bridge can rotate 90 degrees to allow free passage of water traffic. The weight of the mechanical tower balances the weight of the pylon, allowing the rotational system to be simplified. With its night lighting, the bridge has become a symbol for the regeneration of this part of the capital."

1998–2001 ▸ Bodegas Ysios

Laguardia, Spain

The Bodegas & Bebidas Group wanted a building that would be an icon for its prestigious new Rioja Alavesa wine. They called on architect Santiago Calatrava to design an 8,000-square-meter winery complex, a building that had to be designed to make, store, and sell wine. Vineyards occupy half of the rectangular site. A difference in height of 10 meters from the north to the south of the site complicated the design. The linear program of the winemaking process dictated that the structure should be rectangular and it was set along an east-west axis. Two longitudinal concrete load-bearing walls, separated from each other by 26 meters, trace a 196-meter-long sinusoidal shape in plan and in elevation. These walls are covered with wooden planks, which are mirrored in a reflecting pool and "evoke the image of a row of wine barrels." The roof, composed of a series of laminated wood beams, is designed as a continuation of the façades. The result is a "ruled surface wave," which combines concave and convex surfaces as it evolves along the longitudinal axis. The roof is clad in aluminum, creating a contrast with the warmth of the wooden façades and yet continuing their design. A visitor's center conceived as a "balcony that overlooks the winery and the vineyard" is situated in the center of the structure.

Left: The angled windows of the interior room correspond to the high point of the roof, seen from the exterior on the previous double-page.

Opposite page top: The movement of the roof translates into an apparently irregular orchestration of wooden beams in a wine cellar, where barrels are neatly stacked.

Below: Seen in section here is the forward-leaning shape of the room visible above.

Opposite page bottom: The floor plan of the winery reveals a practical and an essentially symmetric plan, although the alternating convex and concave forms seen in the roof is echoed in the main walls.

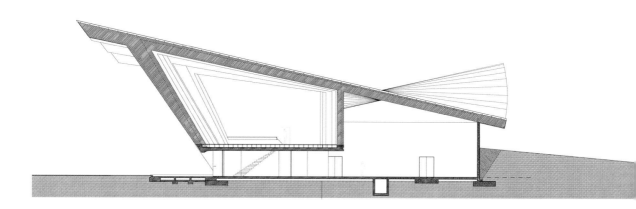

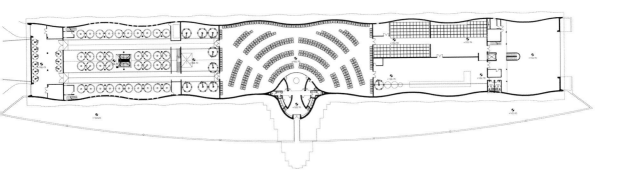

1999–2004 ▸ Turning Torso
Malmö, Sweden

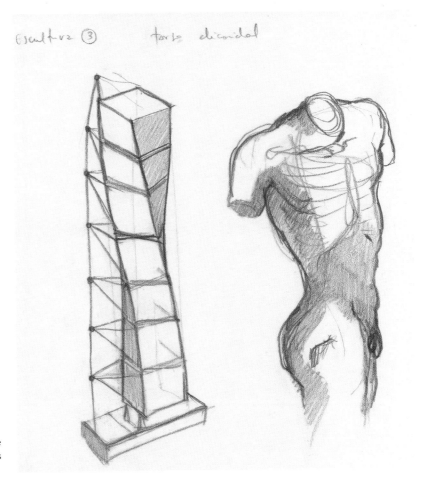

Calatrava's Turning Torso building in Malmö, Sweden (1999–2004), is the result of his intense interest in sculpture, an art he often treats as a study in statics. Calatrava first created a sculpture in which "seven cubes are set around a steel support to produce a spiral structure, which resembles a twisting human spine." As the architect explains the relationship of the tower to the sculpture, "In the Turning Torso building, the spiraling tower is composed of nine box units, each of five floors. The equivalent in the tower of the sculpture's steel support is the nucleus of internal elevators and stairs, through which the box units communicate." The cubes of the original sculpture are replaced by "sub-buildings," each of which has a floor area of approximately 2,200 square meters, with each floor within these boxes accommodating from one to five residence units around the vertical nucleus. Areas in the "spine" are reserved for common facilities, such as meeting rooms or a gym. As is often the case, the engineering used by Calatrava

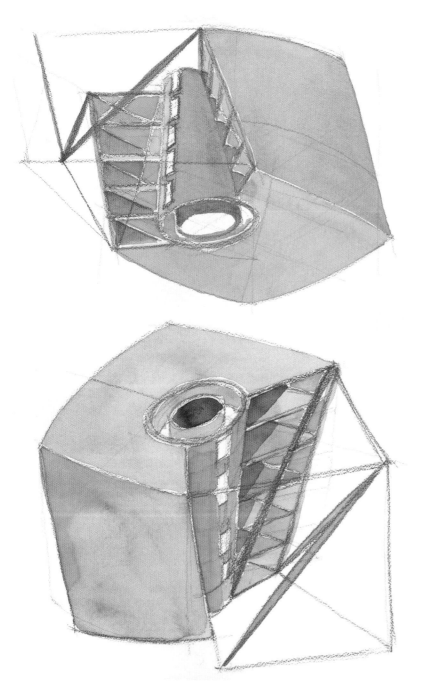

Opposite page: A section of the tower shows the accumulated blocks that form the main structure.

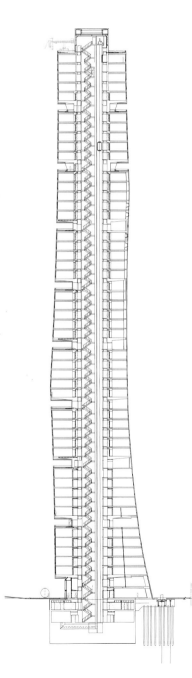

simplified and accelerated construction greatly, relying on prefabricated elements for the exterior steel structure and façade, for example.

2001–2004·Olympic Sports Complex
Athens, Greece

Calatrava's design was intended to deal with the facilities of the existing Athens Olympic Sports Complex (OAKA), located in Marousi, a suburb north of Athens, as well as their infrastructure and access network (subway, commuter rail, highways). As he explains, "The design aimed to meet all the functional requirements of the Olympic and Paralympic Games; to integrate the OAKA's elements aesthetically by providing a common identity through a combination of built and natural elements; to accommodate people with special needs; and to respect the environment through the use of autochthonous plantings (such as olive trees and cypresses), provision of efficient solutions to waste management, and other elements of ecologically sensitive design." The principal architectural interventions were: a new roof for the Olympic Stadium; a new roof and refurbishing of the Velodrome; the creation of entrance plazas and entrance canopies for the complex as a whole; the creation of a central Olympic Icon (a movable steel sculpture in the form of a 110-meter-high spindle); the design of a sculptural Nations' Wall (a 250-meter-long, 20-meter-high tubular steel sculpture); provision of new warm-up areas for athletes; improvement of pedestrian bridges and connections to public transportation; provision of parking areas and bus terminals; and design of the installations and infrastructure for all elements. The most spectacular element is the roof of the Olympic Stadium, covering a surface of 25,000 square meters, with two "bent leaf" structures made of tubular steel and spanning 304

Above: Calatrava created the new suspended roof of the main Olympic Stadium in Athens.

meters each. The structures were designed so that they could be prefabricated off-site to the greatest extent possible, reducing the need for on-site personnel and equipment and minimizing interference with other construction work on the existing buildings.

Above: Interior of the main stadium with Calatrava's spectacular 304-meter-long tubular steel elements visible on either side of the image

Left: Sketches by Calatrava of human figures in movement might be considered an evocation of Olympic sports as much as they are at the origin of specific architectural forms.

Below: The Olympic Velodrome, with curving
tubular steel supports that echo those of the main
stadium

Right: A sketch by the architect shows these
supports and reveals a plan that again draws on
the basic form of the human eye.

Below: A spectacular entrance canopy with the
Velodrome visible to the right

Right: The Nations' Wall, a movable sculpture
designed by the architect for the Games

2002–2007 ▸ 80 South Street Tower

New York, New York, USA

Opposite page: A computer perspective showing the future tower rising above the South Street Seaport on New York's East River

Right: In a lighter vein than usual, Calatrava made a series of sketches of the interiors of the apartments in the South Street Tower.

Santiago Calatrava's first residential project in the United States was born out of a visit to a site in lower Manhattan near the South Street Seaport with the developer Frank Sciame that occurred in the summer of 2002. As was the case for the Turning Torso building in Sweden, the South Street Tower is also connected to the architect's sculptures as well as to his drawings of the human body in movement. The new design is made up of 12 glazed cubes measuring 13.7 meters on each side and containing four floors of residential space. Cantilevered in "steplike fashion" around a vertical core containing technical conduits and elevators, the building will be 254 meters high and contain 16,260 square meters of floor space. The developer's intention has been to lodge a cultural institution in the 5,500-square-meter base of the structure. Aside from the spectacular appearance of the tower as seen from the outside, the cube design has the advantage of offering each floor views of the city and surrounding areas on all four sides.

2003–2009▸World Trade Center Transportation Hub

New York, New York, USA

Opposite page: A computer perspective of the exterior form of the underground station

Right: A perspective of the spectacular underground space

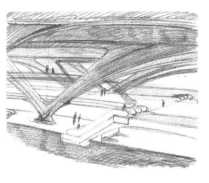

Above: One of a large series of red chalk drawings made by the architect as part of his presentation to the clients

As might be expected given the circumstances, the plans to rebuild the area around the former World Trade Center in New York have been wracked by disagreements and changes, of course. One of the few projects that appears to be advancing as planned originally is that of Santiago Calatrava for a new, permanent transportation hub, designed to serve riders of the Port Authority Trans-Hudson (PATH) commuter trains, New York city subway trains (1/9, E and N/R lines), and a potential rail link to John F. Kennedy International Airport. Set directly to the east of the footprint of the Twin Towers, the work is going forward in collaboration with DMJM + Harris as well as the STV Group. As is almost always the case in Calatrava's work, the Transportation Hub will have a spectacular element—a freestanding arched oval structure made of glass and steel bringing forth the image of "a bird released from a child's hands" at the southern edge of Daniel Libeskind's *Wedge of Light* plaza, and measuring about 106 meters long, 35 meters across at its widest point, and 29 meters high at its apex. As the architect explains, "The steel ribs that support this structure extend upward into a pair of canopies, which resemble outspread wings and rise to a maximum height of 51 meters." The main concourse of the hub is located about 10 meters bottom street level, and the PATH train platforms eight meters lower. In good weather and each September 11, the roof can be opened to the sky. Both the birdlike form and the possibility to open the roof are typical gestures of Calatrava, and yet, in this instance, both take on a particularly poignant and appropriate meaning. Calatrava's ability to deal with the substantial local, state, city, and business bureaucracies involved in each step of the design bears testimony to his emergence as one of the major international architects of the 21st century.

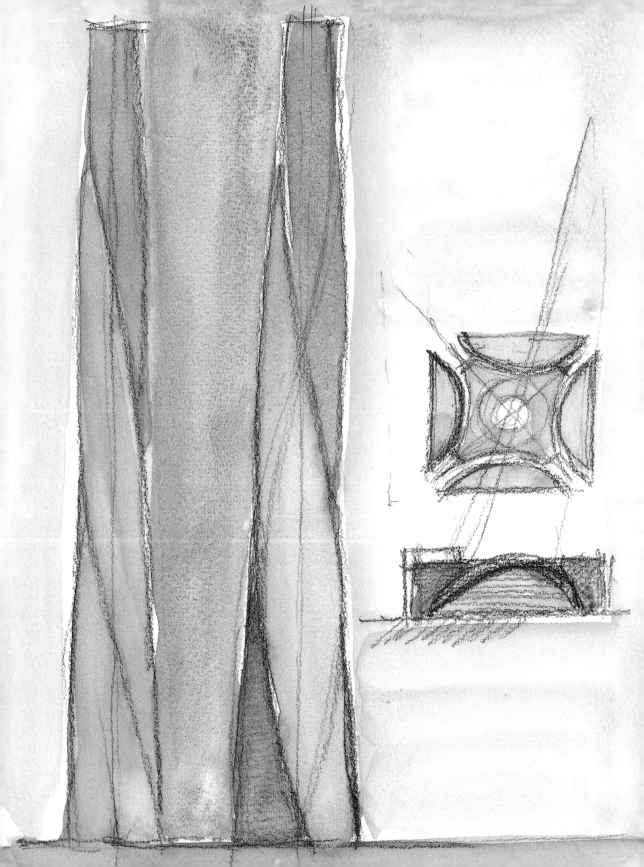

2005–2009 ▸ Chicago Spire
Chicago, Illinois, USA

Above: A computer view of the Chicago skyline with Calatrava's Spire standing far above the city's landmark towers, such as the Sears or John Hancock buildings

Located on North Water Street at Lake Shore Drive, this 610 meters high, 160-story condominium structure will be the tallest building in the United States, as well might seem appropriate in a city that long held the record for the tallest building in the world. Sited on a one-hectare site, the tower was originally to have a footprint of just 1,300 square meters and a gross floor area of 85,500 square meters. Enlarged to include as many as 1,300 condominiums, the new design is broader than the original and has a much higher floor area as well. As the architect's office describes the design, "Based on a sculpture by Santiago Calatrava, the building is a tall, slender elegant form whose glass façade seems to ripple downward in waves, like the folds of a cloak swirling around a figure. This effect is achieved by means of a structural innovation. Each floor unit of the tower is built out from the central core like a separate box, with gently curving, concave sides. As these boxes are stacked up, each is rotated by a little more than two degrees from the one below. In this way, the floors turn 270 degrees around the core as they rise, giving the façade an impression of movement." Floor to ceiling windows and column-free floor plans will allow both hotel and condominium residents to have breathtaking views.

Opposite page: Calatrava's sketches show the symmetry of the core of the building and its twisting exterior shape.

Life and Work

1951 ▸ Santiago Calatrava is born on July 28, 1951, in Valencia, Spain.

1957 ▸ Attends the Arts and Crafts School, Valencia, where he begins his formal instruction in drawing and painting.

1964 ▸ His family takes advantage of the recent opening of the borders and sends him to France as an exchange student.

1968 ▸ Graduates from college in Valencia.

1968–1969 ▸ Attends Art School in Valencia.

1969–1974 ▸ Studies architecture at the Escuela Técnica Superior de Arquitectura, Valencia, where he earns a degree in architecture and takes a postgraduate course in urbanism.

1975–1979 ▸ Postgraduate studies in civil engineering at the ETH (Federal Institute of Technology) in Zurich.

1979 ▸ Marriage.
Cable-stayed bridge studies
Alpine Bridges, Disentis, Switzerland
IBA Squash Complex, Berlin, Germany

1979–1981 ▸ Doctorate in Technical Science from the Department of Architecture ETH Zurich; Ph.D. thesis: "Concerning the Foldability Spaceframes."

1981 ▸ Establishes his own architectural and engineering practice in Zurich.
Züspa Exhibition Hall, Zurich, Switzerland

1982
Letten Motorway Bridge, Zurich, Switzerland
Schwarzhaupt Factory, Dielsdorf, Switzerland
Mühlenareal Library, Thun, Switzerland
Rhine Bridge, Diepoldsau, Switzerland

1983
Thalberg House Balcony Extension, Zurich, Switzerland
Baumwollhof Balcony, Zurich, Switzerland

1983–1984
Jakem Warehouse, Münchwilen, Switzerland

1983–1985
Ernsting's Warehouse, Coesfeld-Lette, Germany
PTT Postal Center Canopy, Lucerne, Switzerland
St. Fiden Bus Shelter, St. Gallen, Switzerland

1983–1988
Wohlen High School Roofs and Hall, Wohlen, Switzerland

1983–1989
Lucerne Station Hall, Lucerne, Switzerland

1983–1990
Stadelhofen Station, Zurich, Switzerland

1984
De Sede Collapsible Exhibition Pavilion, Zurich, Switzerland
Caballeros Footbridge, Lerida, Spain

1984–1985
Dobi Office Building, Suhr, Switzerland

1984–1987 ▸ The Bach de Roda – Felipe II Bridge in Barcelona marks the beginning of the bridge projects that establish his international reputation.
Bach de Roda – Felipe II Bridge, Barcelona, Spain

1984–1988
Bärenmatte Community Center, Suhr, Switzerland

1985 ▸ "9 sculptures" by Santiago Calatrava, exhibition at the Jamileh Weber Gallery, Zurich
Feldenmoos Park & Ride Footbridge, Feldenmoos, Switzerland
Station Square Bus Terminal, Lucerne, Switzerland

1986
Avenida Diagonal Traffic Signal Gantry, Barcelona, Spain
St. Gallen Music School Concert Room, St. Gallen, Switzerland
Raitenau Overpass, Salzburg, Austria

1986–1987
Blackbox Television Studio, Zurich, Switzerland
Tabourettli Theater, Basel, Switzerland

1986–1988
9 de Octubre Bridge, Valencia, Spain

1987
Thiers Pedestrian Bridge, Thiers, France
Pontevedra Bridge, Pontevedra, Spain
Basarrate Metro Station, Bilbao, Spain
Banco Exterior, Zurich, Switzerland
Cascine Footbridge, Florence, Italy

1987–1988
Oudry-Mesly Footbridge, Créteil, France

1987–1992
BCE Place: Gallery & Heritage Square, Toronto, Canada
Alamillo Bridge and La Cartuja Viaduct, Seville, Spain

1987–1996
Buchen Housing Estate, Würenlingen, Switzerland

1988
Pré Babel Sports Center, Geneva, Switzerland
Leimbach Footbridge and Station, Zurich, Switzerland
Collserola Communications Tower, Barcelona, Spain
Wettstein Bridge, Basel, Switzerland
Gentil Bridge, Paris, France
Bauschänzli Restaurant, Zurich, Switzerland

1988–1991
Lusitania Bridge, Merida, Spain

1988–1999
Emergency Services Center, St. Gallen, Switzerland

1989 ► Establishes second office, in Paris.
Miraflores Bridge, Cordoba, Spain
Bahnhofquai Tram Stop, Zurich, Switzerland
Reuss Footbridge, Flüelen, Switzerland
Swissbau Concrete Pavilion, Basel, Switzerland
Muri Monastery Old Age Home, Muri, Switzerland
CH-91 Floating Concrete Pavilion, Lake Lucerne, Switzerland
Gran Via Bridge, Barcelona, Spain
Port de la Lune Swingbridge, Bordeaux, France

1989–1991
La Devesa Footbridge, Ripoll, Spain

1989–1992
Montjuic Communications Tower, Barcelona, Spain

1989–1994
Lyon-Saint Exupéry Airport Railway Station, Satolas, France

1989–1995
Puerto Bridge, Ondarroa, Spain

1989–1996
Bohl Bus and Tram Stop, St. Gallen, Switzerland

1989–2004
Zurich University – Law Faculty Library, Zurich, Switzerland

1990
Spitalfields Gallery, London, Great Britain
East London River Crossing, London, Great Britain
New Bridge over the Vecchio, Corsica, France
Belluard Castle Theater, Fribourg, Switzerland

1990–2000
Sondica Airport and Control Tower, Bilbao, Spain

1991 ► Opens his third office, in Valencia.
Calabria Football Stadium, Reggio Calabria, Italy
Valencia Communications Tower, Valencia, Spain
Salou Football Stadium, Salou, Spain
Grand Pont, Lille, France
Cathedral of St. John the Divine, New York, New York, USA
Médoc Swingbridge, Bordeaux, France
Betongforum Standard Bridge, Stockholm, Sweden
Spandau Railway Station, Berlin, Germany
Klosterstrasse Railway Viaduct, Berlin, Germany

1991–1992
Kuwait Pavilion, Seville, Spain

1991–1995
Alameda Bridge and Subway Station, Valencia, Spain

1991–1996
Kronprinzen Bridge, Berlin, Germany
Oberbaum Bridge, Berlin, Germany

1991–2000
City of Arts and Sciences, Valencia, Spain

1991–2003
Tenerife Auditorium, Santa Cruz de Tenerife, Spain

1992 ► Retrospective at the Royal Institute of British Architects, London.
Jahn Olympic Sports Complex, Berlin, Germany
Solférino Footbridge, Paris, France
Modular Station, London, Great Britain
Reichstag Conversion, Berlin, Germany
Lake Bridge, Lucerne, Switzerland
Serpis Bridge, Alcoy, Spain

1992–1993
Shadow Machine, New York, New York, USA

1992–1995
Tenerife Exhibition Site, Santa Cruz de Tenerife, Spain
Remodeling of Plaza de España, Alcoy, Spain

1992–
Serreria Bridge, Valencia, Spain

1993 ► Exhibition "Structure and Expression" at The Museum of Modern Art, New York.
Öresund Link, Copenhagen, Denmark
Ile Falcon Viaduct, Sierre, Switzerland
Granadilla Bridge, Tenerife, Spain
De la Rade Bridge, Geneva, Switzerland
Alicante Communications Tower, Alicante, Spain
Roosevelt Island Southpoint Pavilion, New York, New York, USA
Herne Hill Stadium, London, Great Britain

1993–1995
Trinity Footbridge, Salford-Manchester, Great Britain

1993–1996
Sondica Control Tower, Bilbao, Spain

1993–1998
Oriente Station, Lisbon, Portugal

1993–1999
Hospital Bridges, Murcia, Spain

1994
St Paul's Footbridge, London, Great Britain
Quaypoint Pedestrian Bridge, Bristol, Great Britain
Michelangelo Trade Fair and Convention Center, Fiuggi, Italy

1994–1997
Campo Volantín Footbridge, Bilbao, Spain

1994–1999
Manrique Footbridge, Murcia, Spain

1994–2001
Milwaukee Art Museum, Milwaukee, Wisconsin, USA

1995
Velodrome Football Stadium, Marseille, France
Zurich Station Roof, Zurich, Switzerland
KL Linear City, Kuala Lumpur, Malaysia
Poole Harbour Bridge, Portsmouth, Great Britain
Embankment Renaissance Footbridge, Bedford, Great Britain
Sundsvall Bridge, Sundsvall, Sweden
Bilbao Football Stadium, Bilbao, Spain

1995–2004
Sundial Footbridge, Redding, California, USA

1996
Olympic Stadium, Stockholm, Sweden
Church of the Year 2000, Rome, Italy
Cathedral Square, Los Angeles, California, USA
City Point, London, Great Britain
Porte de la Suisse Motorway Service Area,
Geneva, Switzerland

1996–1998
Mimico Creek Pedestrian Bridge, Toronto, Canada

1996–2000
Pont de l'Europe, Orléans, France

1996–2006
Opera House, Valencia, Spain

1996–2007
Liège-Guillemins TGV Railway Station, Liège,
Belgium

1996–
Quarto Ponte sul Canal Grande, Venice, Italy

1997
Port de Barcelona, Barcelona, Spain
Barajas Airport, Madrid, Spain

1997–1999
Pfalzkeller Gallery, St. Gallen, Switzerland

1998
Pennsylvania Railway Station, New York, New
York, USA
Toronto Island Airport Bridge, Toronto, Canada

1998–2000
Pont des Guillemins, Liège, Belgium

1998–2001
Mujer Bridge, Buenos Aires, Argentina
Bodegas Ysios, Laguardia, Spain

1998–2003
Petah-Tikva Footbridge, Tel Aviv, Israel
Samuel Beckett (Macken Street) Bridge and
James Joyce Bridge, Dublin, Ireland

1998–
Woodall Rodgers Bridges, Dallas, Texas, USA
IH-30 Bridge, Dallas, Texas, USA
IH-35 Bridge, Dallas, Texas, USA

1999
Wildbachstrasse, Zurich, Switzerland
The Corcoran Gallery of Art, Washington DC, USA
Nova Ponte Sobre o Rio Cavado, Barcelos, Portugal
Pedestrian Bridge, Pistoia, Italy
Rouen Bridge, Rouen, France
Cruz y Luz, Monterrey, Mexico
Saragossa Station, Saragossa, Spain
Residential House, Phoenix, Arizona, USA
Leuven Station, Sint-Niklaas, Belgium
Reina Sofia National Museum of Art, Madrid, Spain

1999–2004
Turning Torso, Malmö, Sweden
Bridges over the Hoofdvaart, Hoofddorp, The
Netherlands

2000
Christ the Light Cathedral, Oakland, California, USA
Opera House Parking, Zurich, Switzerland
Dallas Fort Worth Airport, Dallas, Texas, USA
Ryerson Polytechnic University, Toronto, Canada
Darsena del Puerto, Centro Municipal, Torrevieja,
Spain
Kornhaus, Rorschach, Switzerland
Zurich Stadium, Zurich, Switzerland
SMU's Meadows Museum Wave Sculpture,
Dallas, Texas, USA
Ciudad de la Porcelana, Valencia, Spain

2000–
Crati Bridge, Cosenza, Italy
Buenavista and Jovellanos, Oviedo, Spain
University Campus Buildings and Sports Hall,
Maastricht, The Netherlands

2001
The American Museum of Natural History, New
York, New York, USA
Queens Landing Pedestrian Access Improvement,
Chicago, Illinois, USA
Las Troyanas Stage Setting, Valencia, Spain
Neratziotissa Metro and Railway Station, Athens,
Greece
Private residence, Qatar
The New York Times Capsule, New York, New
York, USA
Lake Promenade, Rorschach, Switzerland

2001–2002 ▶ "Santiago Calatrava: Artist,
Architect, Engineer", presented at Palazzo Strozzi
in Florence, Italy.

2001–2004
Olympic Sports Complex, Athens, Greece
Katehaki Pedestrian Bridge, Athens, Greece

2002
Vittoria Bridge, Florence, Italy
Reconstruction of the Museum of the Opera di
S. Maria del Fiore, Florence, Italy

2002–2003
Ecuba Stage Setting, Rome, Italy

2002–2007
80 South Street Tower, New York, New York, USA

2002–
Reggio-Emilia, Bologna, Italy
Atlanta Symphony Center, Atlanta, Georgia, USA
Light Rail Train (LRT) Bridge, Jerusalem, Israel
Photography Museum Doha, Qatar
New High-Speed Railway Station, Florence, Italy
Greenpoint Landing, New York, New York, USA

2003 ▶ Exhibition "Like a Bird" held at the Kunst-
historisches Museum in Vienna, Austria.

2003–2009
World Trade Center Transportation Hub, New
York, New York, USA

2003–
Lake Shore Drive, Chicago, Illinois, USA

2004
Railway and Automobile Bridge, Kiev, Ukraine

2004–
Valencia Towers, Valencia, Spain
Obelisk Plaza Castilla, Madrid, Spain

2005 ▶ Solo exhibitions in New York about his
work as an artist, one at the Metropolitan
Museum of Art titled "Santiago Calatrava:
Sculpture into Architecture" and another at the
Queen Sofia Spanish Institute, "Clay and Paint:
Ceramics and Watercolors."
International Fair World Expo, Thessaloniki, Greece

2005–2009
Chicago Spire, Chicago, Illinois, USA

2005–
Agora, Valencia, Spain
City of Sports Tor Vergata, Law Faculty and
Rectory University Tor Vergata, Rome, Italy

2006–
Governors Island Gondola, New York, New York,
USA
Science House, Zurich, Switzerland

World Map

Argentina
Buenos Aires
Mujer Bridge

France
Satolas
Lyon-Saint Exupéry Airport Railway Station

Germany
Coesfeld-Lette
Ernsting's Warehouse

Greece
Athens
Olympic Sports Complex

Portugal
Lisbon
Oriente Station

Spain
Barcelona
Montjuic Communications Tower
Bach de Roda–Felipe II Bridge
Bilbao
Sondica Airport and Control Tower
Campo Volantín Footbridge
Laguardia
Bodegas Ysios
Santa Cruz de Tenerife, Canary Islands
Tenerife Auditorium
Seville
Alamillo Bridge and La Cartuja Viaduct
Valencia
City of Arts and Sciences / Opera House

Sweden
Malmö
Turning Torso

Switzerland
Zurich
Stadelhofen Station

USA
Chicago, Illinois
Chicago Spire
Milwaukee, Wisconsin
Milwaukee Art Museum
New York, New York
80 South Street Tower
World Trade Center Transportation Hub

SWEDEN

Malmö

Coesfeld-Lette

GERMANY

FRANCE ● SWITZERLAND

Zurich

Bilbao   Satolas

Laguardia   Barcelona

PORTUGAL

Lisbon   SPAIN   Valencia

Seville

GREECE

Athens

z de Tenerife

Bibliography

Credits

▶ Blanco, Manuel: *Santiago Calatrava*. Exhibition catalogue. Valencia: Generalitat Valenciana, 1999
▶ Blaser, Werner: *Santiago Calatrava Ingenieur-Architektur*. Basel: Birkhäuser, 1987
▶ Calatrava, Santiago: *Calatrava Alpine Bridges*. Weinfelden: Wolfau-Druck AG, 2004
▶ El Croquis: *Santiago Calatrava 1983–1993*. Exhibition catalogue. Madrid: El Croquis, 1993
▶ Fernández-Galiano, Luis: *Santiago Calatrava 1983–1996*. AV Monografías/Monographs 61 (1996). Madrid: *Arquitectura Viva*, 1996
▶ Frampton, Kenneth/Webster, Anthony C./Tischhauser, Anthony: *Santiago Calatrava: Bridges*. Zurich: Birkhäuser, 1993
▶ Harrison, Robert: *Creatures from the Mind of the Engineer: The Architecture of Santiago Calatrava*. Zurich: Artemis, 1992
▶ Jodidio, Philip: *Estaçao do Oriente, Estacion de Oriente, Oriente Station*. Lisbon: Centralivros Lda, 1998
▶ Jodidio, Philip: *Santiago Calatrava*. Cologne: Taschen, 1998
▶ Jodidio, Philip: *Santiago Calatrava*. Cologne: Taschen, 2003
▶ Kent, Cheryl: *Santiago Calatrava: Milwaukee Art Museum Quadracci Pavilion*. New York: Rizzoli, 2005
▶ Levene, Richard C./Cecilia, Fernando Márquez: *Santiago Calatrava 1983/1989*. Madrid: El Croquis, 1989
▶ Levin, Michael: Calatrava. *Drawings and Sculptures*. Exhibition catalogue. Weinfelden: Wolfau-Druck Rudolf Mühlemann, 2000
▶ Levin, Michael: *Santiago Calatrava: Artworks*. Basel: Birkhäuser, 2003
▶ McQuaid, Matilda: *Santiago Calatrava: Structure and Expression*. Exhibition catalogue. New York: The Museum of Modern Art, 1992
▶ Nicolin, Pierluigi: *Santiago Calatrava: Il folle volo/The daring flight*. Milan: Electa, 1987
▶ Pisani, Mario/Sicignano, Enrico/Mandolesi, Domizia: *Santiago Calatrava*. Rome: Progetti e Opere, 1997
▶ Polano, Sergio: *Santiago Calatrava: Complete Works*. Exhibition catalogue. Milan: Electa, 1996
▶ Sharp, Dennis: *Santiago Calatrava*. Exhibition catalogue. London, 1992
▶ Sharp, Dennis: *Santiago Calatrava*. Architectural Monographs No 46. London: Academy Editions, 1996
▶ Tischhauser, Anthony/Moos, Stanislaus von: *Santiago Calatrava: Public Buildings*. Basel: Birkhäuser, 1998
▶ Trame, Umberto: *OP/O Opera Progetto Santiago Calatrava: Quadracci Pavilion, Milwaukee Art Museum*. Bologna: Editrice Compositori, 2001
▶ Tzonis, Alexander: *Santiago Calatrava: The Poetics of Movement*. New York: Universe Publishing, 1999
▶ Tzonis, Alexander: *Santiago Calatrava: Creative Process: Fundamentals*. Basel: Birkhäuser, 2001
▶ Tzonis, Alexander: *Santiago Calatrava: The Complete Works*. New York: Rizzoli, 2004
▶ Tzonis, Alexander: *Santiago Calatrava: The Athens Olympics*. New York: Rizzoli, 2005
▶ Tzonis, Alexander/Caso Dondei, Rebecca: *Santiago Calatrava: The Bridges*. New York: Rizzoli, 2005
▶ Tzonis, Alexander/Lefaivre, Liane: *Movement, Structure and the Work of Santiago Calatrava*. Basel: Birkhäuser, 1995
▶ Tzonis, Alexander/Lefaivre, Liane: *Santiago Calatrava: Creative Process: Sketchbooks*. Basel: Birkhäuser, 2001
▶ Zardini, Mirco: *Santiago Calatrava: Secret Sketchbook*. Milan: Federico Motta Editore, 1995

The Author

Philip Jodidio studied art history and economics at Harvard University, and was the Editor-in-Chief of the French art journal *Connaissance des Arts* from 1980–2002. He has published numerous articles and books, including TASCHEN's *Architecture Now!* series, *Building a New Millennium*, and monographs on Norman Foster, Richard Meier, Álvaro Siza, Tadao Ando, and Renzo Piano.